# Fingerpower®
## Primer Level

*Effective Technic for All Piano Methods*

### By John W. Schaum
**Edited by Wesley Schaum**

## FOREWORD

Strong fingers are an important requirement for all pianists, amateur and professional. Schaum Fingerpower® exercises are designed to strengthen all five fingers of both hands.

Equal hand development is assured by the performance of the same patterns in each hand. The exercises are short and easily memorized. This enables the student to focus his/her efforts on technical benefits, listening attentively, and playing with a steady beat.

A measure number (enclosed in a small box) is included at the beginning of each system of music. This makes it easier to locate measures during the lesson and for written practice assignments.

The exercises become progressively more difficult as the student moves through the book. This makes the exercises an ideal companion to a method book at the same level.

The Primer Level of Fingerpower® may be started after only six to eight weeks of study.

The series consists of seven books, Primer Level through Level 6.

To access audio, visit:
**www.halleonard.com/mylibrary**

4409-0962-5555-9063

ISBN 978-1-4950-8198-9

EXCLUSIVELY DISTRIBUTED BY

Visit Hal Leonard Online at
**www.halleonard.com**

Contact us:
**Hal Leonard**
7777 West Bluemound Road
Milwaukee, WI 53213
Email: info@halleonard.com

In Europe, contact:
**Hal Leonard Europe Limited**
42 Wigmore Street
Marylebone, London, W1U 2RN
Email: info@halleonardeurope.com

In Australia, contact:
**Hal Leonard Australia Pty. Ltd.**
4 Lentara Court
Cheltenham, Victoria, 3192 Australia
Email: info@halleonard.com.au

# CONTENTS

## PRACTICE SUGGESTIONS

To derive the full benefit from these exercises, they should be played with a firm, solid finger action. **Listen carefully while practicing**. Try to play **each finger equally loud**. Each hand should also play equally loud. It is also important to be aware of the feeling in your fingers and hands during practice.

Each exercise should be practiced four or five times daily, starting at a slow tempo and gradually increasing the tempo as proficiency improves. Several previously learned exercises should be reviewed each week as part of regular practice.

## ABOUT THE AUDIO

To access the accompanying audio, go to **www.halleonard.com/mylibrary** and enter the code found on the first page of this book. This will grant you instant access to every example.

There are two tracks for each exercise:
1. Slow practice tempo
2. Performance tempo

The solo part is emphasized on the practice track. The accompaniment is emphasized on the performance track. For the *Primer Level*, the accompaniments are purposely kept very simple so as not to distract the student. The exercise is played twice on each practice track. There are two extra count-in measures before each track.

Follow these three steps for practice variety. At first, the steps should be done with the slow practice tempo. The same steps may be used again at the performance tempo.
1. Student plays right hand only
2. Student plays left hand only
3. Student plays both hands together

# 1. Two-Finger Legato (2/4)

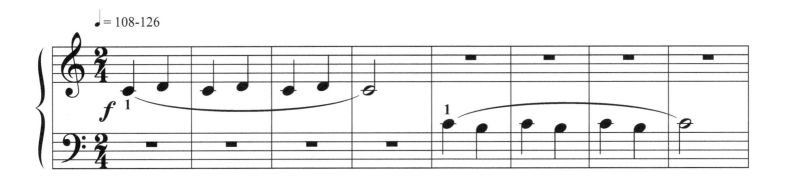

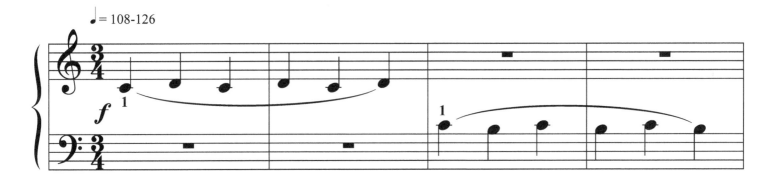

# 2. Two-Finger Legato (3/4)

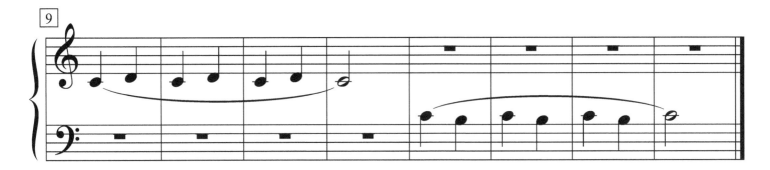

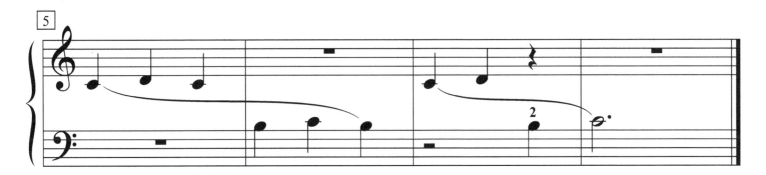

**Teacher's Note**: Phrase marks are intended to show groups of notes that form patterns. Some of these patterns recur. The student should be shown how to recognize patterns which are the same.

It is recommended that all studies in this book be played *forte* with firm finger articulation. There is a well-known motto: "He who can do the most, can do the least." In other words, strong fingers can play softly, but weak fingers cannot perform with clarity.

# 3. Three-Finger Legato (4/4)

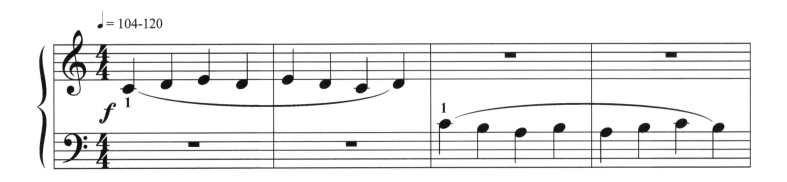

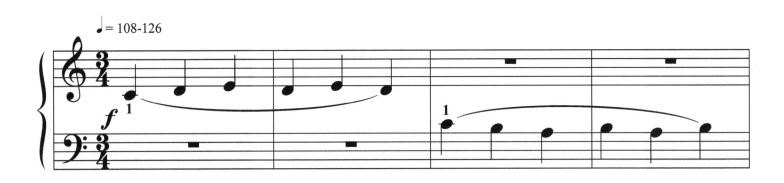

# 4. Three-Finger Legato (3/4)

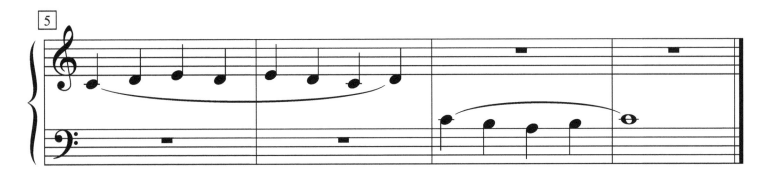

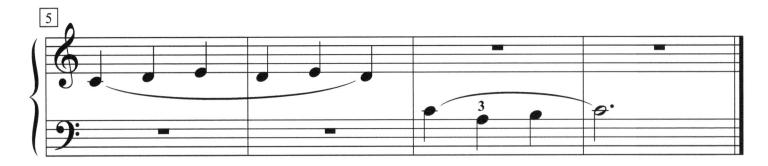

5

## 5. Four-Finger Legato (4/4)

## 6. Four-Finger Legato (3/4)

# 7. Five-Finger Legato (4/4)

# 8. Five-Finger Legato (3/4)

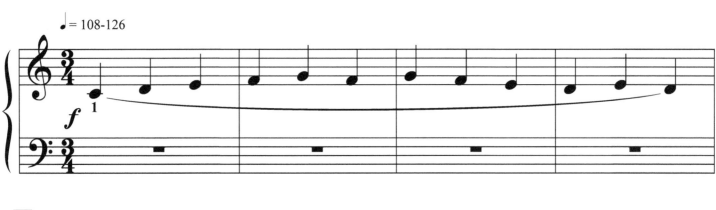

# 9. Broken Thirds (4/4)

# 10. Broken Thirds (3/4)

# 11. Blocked Thirds

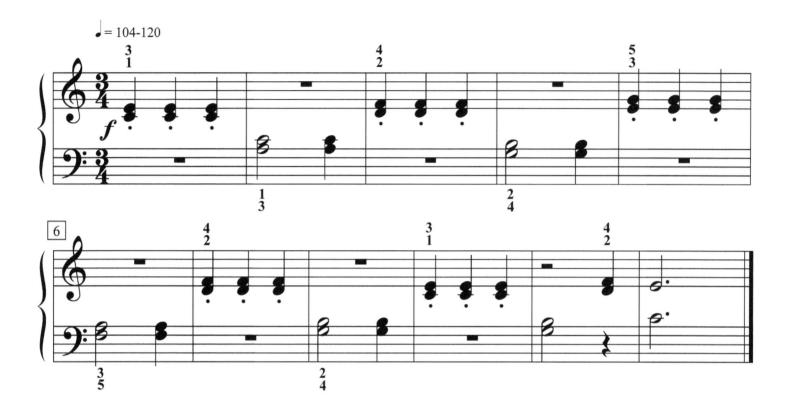

# 12. Mixed Intervals (4/4)

# 13. Mixed Intervals (3/4)

# 14. Interval Phrasing

## 15. Left Hand Melody (Broken Accompaniment)

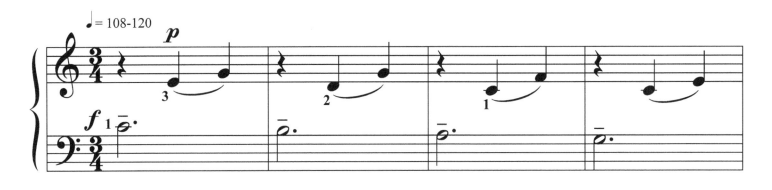

## 16. Left Hand Melody (Blocked Accompaniment)

**Review Practice.** One or two previously learned exercises should be played as part of daily practice. Try to improve by keeping the rhythm very steady and gradually increasing the tempo.

# 17. Right Hand Melody (Broken Accompaniment)

# 18. Right Hand Melody (Blocked Accompaniment)

# 19. Quarter Notes and Eighth Notes

# 20. Legato and Staccato

# 21. Eighth Notes with Staccato

# 22. Thumb Crossings

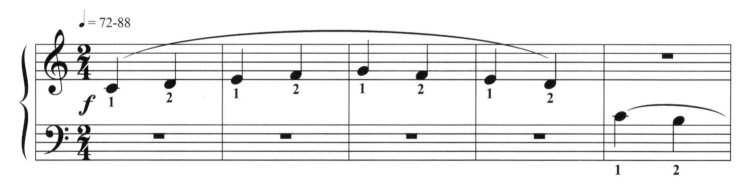

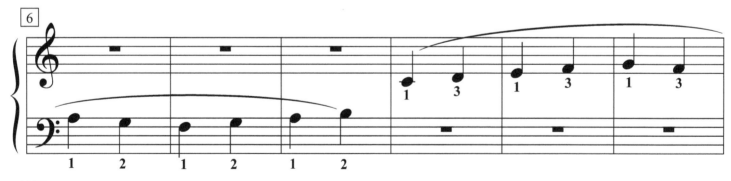

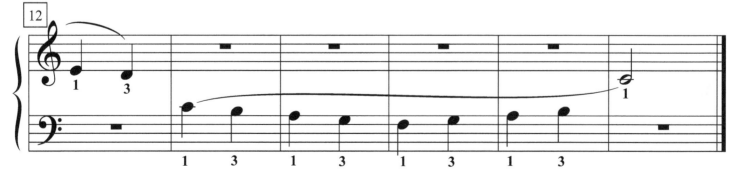

# 23. Sharps and Flats

# 24. Sharps and Flats (Chromatic)

Notice that this entire exercise uses only the 1st and 3rd fingers of both hands.

# 25. Cross Hands (Bass and Treble)

*L.H.* = Left Hand.   *R.H.* = Right Hand.   Notice that only the 3rd finger is used in both hands throughout this exercise.

# 26. Cross Hands (Three C's)

*The first *quarter note* of this exercise is **bass C**, one octave *below* middle C. The first *half note* is **treble C**, one octave *above* middle C.

# 27. Triads (Broken and Blocked)

# 28. Triad Exploration

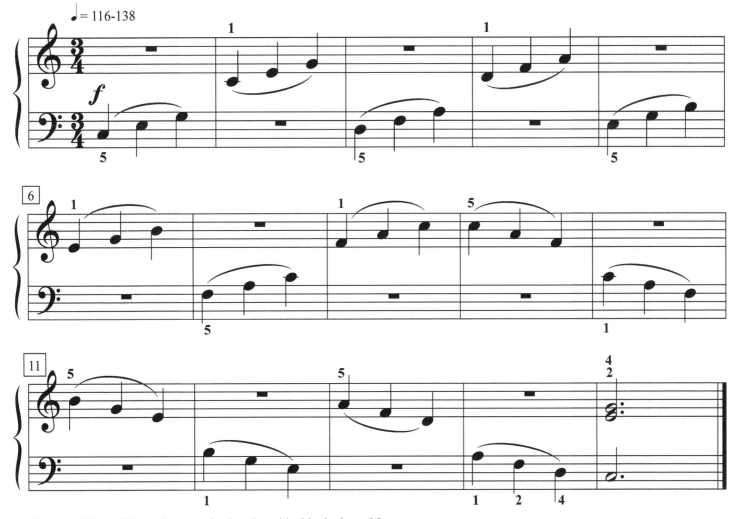

Teacher's Note: This study may also be played in *blocked triad* form.

# 29. Two-Note Phrases

Optional work: This exercise may also be played with different finger patterns: 1-2, 3-4, and 4-5

# 30. Three-Note Phrases

Optional work: This exercise may also be played with different finger patterns: 1-2-3, and 3-4-5.

# 31. Four-Note Phrases

Optional work: This exercise may also be played with a different finger pattern: 1-2-3-4.

# 32. Two-Finger Extensions

Optional work: This exercise may also be played with different finger patterns: 2-3, 3-4 and 4-5.

# *33. Parallel Motion (4/4)

# *34. Parallel Motion (3/4)

* Parallel motion is the movement of two melodies in the same direction. In these exercises, right hand and left hand go up and down at the same time, playing the same notes one octave apart.

# *35. Contrary Motion (4/4)

# *36. Contrary Motion (3/4)

*Contrary motion is the movement of two melodies in **opposite** directions. In these two exercises, if one hand goes up, the other hand goes down and vice-versa. (In both exercises, movement into the last measure is in *parallel* motion to make the ending sound more final.)

***You are now ready to progress to Schaum Fingerpower®, Level 1***

# Reference Page

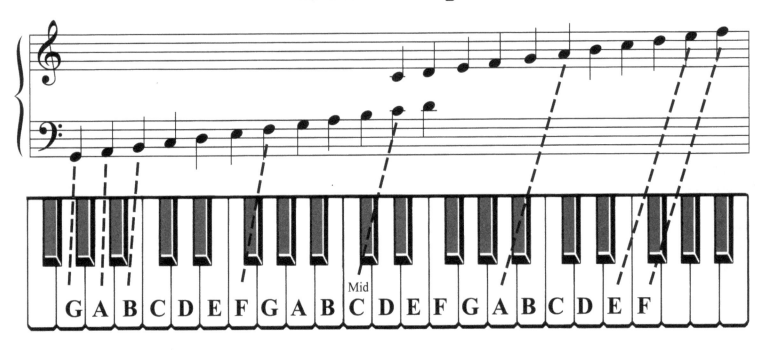

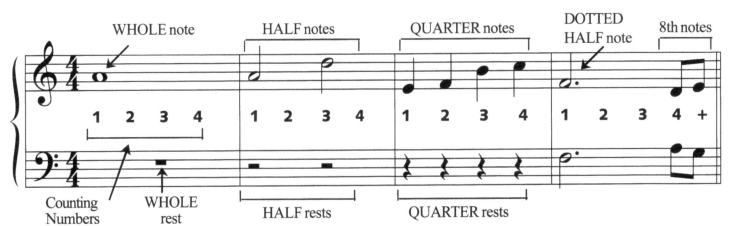

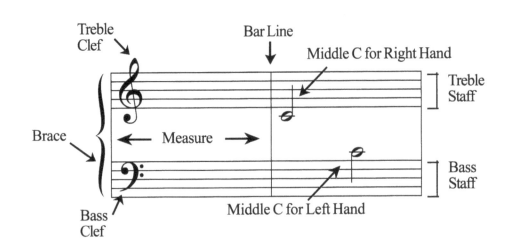

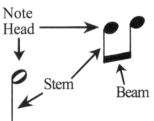

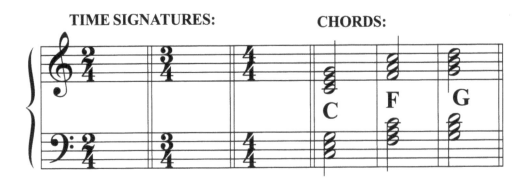